Latino Legends

Hispanics in Major League Baseball

by Michael Silverstone

Reading Consultant:
Timothy Rasinski, Ph.D.
Professor of Reading Education
Kent State University

Content Consultant:
Doran "Duke" Goldman
Lecturer at UMASS-Amherst
Society for American Baseball Research

Red Brick™ Learning

Published by Red Brick™ Learning
7825 Telegraph Road, Bloomington, Minnesota 55438
http://www.redbricklearning.com

Library of Congress Cataloging-in-Publication Data
Silverstone, Michael.
    Latino legends: Hispanics in major league baseball / by Michael Silverstone.
    p. cm.—(High five reading)
    Summary: Profiles some of baseball's present and past superstars who are
from Spanish-speaking countries such as Cuba, Venezuela, and Puerto Rico,
including Roberto Clemente, the Alou brothers, and Miguel Tejada.
Includes bibliographical references and index.
    ISBN 0-7368-2791-9 (hard)—ISBN 0-7368-2832-X (pbk.)
    1. Hispanic American baseball players—Biography—Juvenile literature.
2. Baseball players—Latin America—Biography—Juvenile literature.
3. Baseball—United States—History—Juvenile literature. [1. Baseball players.
2. Hispanic Americans—Biography. 3. Baseball—History.] I. Title. II. Series.
GV865.A1S5153 2003
796.357'092'368073—dc21

                            2003009761

Created by Kent Publishing Services, Inc.
Designed by Signature Design Group, Inc.
This publisher has made every effort to trace ownership of all copyrighted
material and to secure necessary permissions. In the event of any questions
arising as to the use of any material, the publisher, while expressing regret for
any inadvertent error, will be happy to make necessary corrections.

Photo Credits:
Cover, AI Wire Service; page 4, Dave Kennedy/iPhoto, Inc.; pages 8, 10, 13, 16,
18, 20, 23 (middle), 23 (right), 24, 26, 29, 31, 32, 33, Bettmann/Corbis; page
23 (left), Associated Press/A; page 25, AFP/Corbis; page 28, Otto Lang/Corbis;
page 34, Justin Sullivan/Reuters Photo Archive; page 37, Tom Bean/Corbis;
page 39, Barry Taylor/AI Wire Service; page 40, Ana Martinez/Reuters
Photo Archive

Printed in the United States of America.

1 2 3 4 5 6 08 07 06 05 04 03

Table of Contents

Chapter 1

Closed Doors

"Miguel Tejada is the greatest player ever!" Luis told his grandfather.

"Not so fast, mi hijo," Grandfather said. "He's good, but he has a long way to go."

"Then who is the best, Abuelo?"

Miguel Tejada (mi-GELL tay-HA-dah)

---

mi hijo (mee EE-hoh): Spanish for *my boy*
Abuelo (uh-BWAY-loh): Spanish for *grandfather*

The Best in His League

Miguel Tejada dug in at home plate. It was the ninth inning. His team, the Oakland Athletics, was down by two runs. Pitching was the ace closer for the Minnesota Twins.

For most teams, this would have been a lost game. But most teams didn't have Miguel Tejada.

The pitch was a low fastball. With a hard, quick swing, Tejada smashed it into the left-field seats for a 3-run home run. As Tejada ran the base paths, he looked up to the seats to see his dad jumping up and down for joy.

Tejada's 3-run blast won the game. That 2002 season, Tejada also was named the American League MVP. The skinny, poor kid from Latin America had come a long way! Tejada is not the first Latino baseball superstar, however. In fact, the first Latino legends ran the base paths long before Tejada was even born.

---

ace closer: a team's best relief pitcher
MVP (Most Valuable Player): an award given to a very important player

Latino Stars

Miguel Tejada grew up in the Dominican Republic. Today, many stars in major league baseball come from countries where Spanish is the main language. The map below shows the countries where a number of these major league players were born.

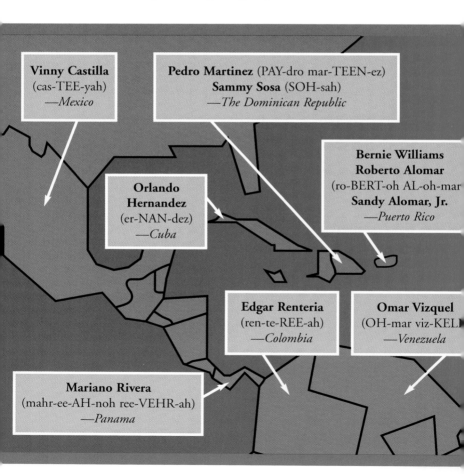

Vinny Castilla (cas-TEE-yah)
—*Mexico*

Pedro Martinez (PAY-dro mar-TEEN-ez)
Sammy Sosa (SOH-sah)
—*The Dominican Republic*

Bernie Williams
Roberto Alomar (ro-BERT-oh AL-oh-mar)
Sandy Alomar, Jr.
—*Puerto Rico*

Orlando Hernandez (er-NAN-dez)
—*Cuba*

Edgar Renteria (ren-te-REE-ah)
—*Colombia*

Omar Vizquel (OH-mar viz-KEL)
—*Venezuela*

Mariano Rivera (mahr-ee-AH-noh ree-VEHR-ah)
—*Panama*

Spreading the Game

Baseball began in the United States in the mid-1800s. This great game soon spread to other countries. In 1864, Nemesio Guillot, a Cuban who went to school in the United States, came home to Cuba with a bat and ball. He taught others there how to play. In 1866, some U.S. sailors played a Cuban team. Interest in baseball spread fast. Professional and amateur teams formed across Cuba.

The game soon took root in other Latin countries, such as Panama and Venezuela. U.S. sailors and workers who lived in these countries spread baseball. By the 1920s, teams in many Latin countries began to play each other.

Nemesio Guillot: (neh-MESS-ee-oh gee-YOH)

professional: done by people who are paid to play
amateur: done by people who play for fun, not money
take root: begin and start to grow

A Cuban Star in the United States

Beginning with Esteban Bellán in 1871, a few Cubans began to play as professionals in the United States. The most famous Cuban player was Adolfo Luque.

Luque joined the Cincinnati Reds in 1914. Even though he was a fine pitcher, fans yelled insults at him. Players did, too. Luque was disliked because he was Cuban, just like the first African American players would later be booed in the 1940s.

Their anger could not stop Luque. The boos and insults only made him play harder. In 1923, he won 27 games—one of the best single-season win totals for a pitcher.

Adolfo Luque

Esteban Bellán: (ES-tuh-bahn beh-YAHN)
Adolfo Luque: (uh-DOLL-foh LU-kay)

---

insult: a hurtful remark

8

Times Change

In the 1940s, two things helped more Latinos play baseball in the United States. The first was World War II (1939–1945). Many U.S. players left baseball to fight in the war. The major leagues had to look for good players in new places.

Also, before 1947, major league baseball had a "color line." Only white players could play in the league. African Americans and other non-whites were not allowed. Latinos with light skin could play, but fans and even other players often booed and insulted them anyway.

Then in 1947, the Brooklyn Dodgers signed an African American player to their team. His name was Jackie Robinson. Other teams then began to sign non-white players. The door was now open to Latino players with darker skin as well.

— CHAPTER **2** —

A New Era

"So Abuelo, was Adolfo Luque the best pitcher ever?"

"I couldn't tell you, Luis. He played in a different time. You can't compare then to now. They didn't always let the best players play back then."

"When did they get their chance?"

"Now that is an interesting story."

Orestes "Minnie" Miñoso

The Cuban Comet

Jackie Robinson was the first African American to play in a major league game. Cuban-born Orestes "Minnie" Miñoso was the first Latino of African descent to play in the majors. Miñoso got his break with the Chicago White Sox in May 1951.

Miñoso thrilled fans from his first big league at bat—he hit a home run. But home runs were not what he did best. He crashed into outfield walls to make impossible catches. He ran so fast he drove other teams crazy as they tried to tag him out. Miñoso had skill, speed, and desire.

Orestes Miñoso (or-ES-tees min-YO-soh)

---

descent: ancestry
desire: a strong wish

Working His Way Up

Miñoso began in the majors with the Cleveland Indians in 1949. But Cleveland had many good outfielders, so they traded him to the Chicago White Sox. That was a lucky day for Chicago baseball fans.

A Long Journey

It took a long time for Miñoso to finally get to play, though. He was a 29-year-old rookie when he joined the White Sox in 1951. Many players join the majors as young as 20.

As a boy in Cuba, Miñoso had dreamed of being a star in U.S. baseball. When dark-skinned Latinos were finally allowed to play in 1947, Miñoso had his chance. But a question remained. Could he hit major league pitching?

---

outfielder: the player whose job is to catch the ball near the back of the field
rookie: a first-year player in a league

Cuba's Orestes Miñoso brought speed and excitement to baseball. Fans gave him the nickname the "Cuban Comet." Miñoso played for the Chicago White Sox.

Blazing a Trail

Miñoso was a great base stealer. In fact, he led the American League in stolen bases for three years in a row. He also led the league in triples several of the years he played. The Chicago fans loved him. More fans now came to games than ever before.

At the end of Miñoso's first season, the team held a special day at the ballpark to thank him. They gave him a new car and the deed to a piece of land in Chicago. He had found a home in the United States.

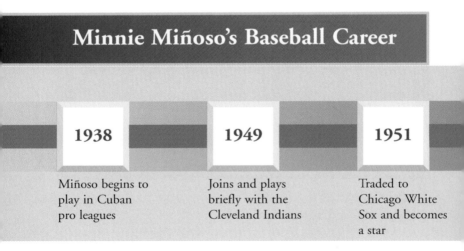

Minnie Miñoso's Baseball Career

1938
Miñoso begins to play in Cuban pro leagues

1949
Joins and plays briefly with the Cleveland Indians

1951
Traded to Chicago White Sox and becomes a star

triple: when a player reaches third base on a hit
deed: paper that shows that someone owns land

Not Always Easy

Miñoso was a baseball hero. But there were hard times, too. In eight seasons, he was hit by pitches more than any other player in the league. Pitchers often hit him on purpose.

Some said Miñoso was so good, it made other players look bad. They didn't like it. But their poor sportsmanship only made him play better.

Miñoso was proud to be a major league player. He was also proud of being Latino. "Every time I put on the uniform I respected it like it was the American flag. I wore it like I was representing every Latin country," he said.

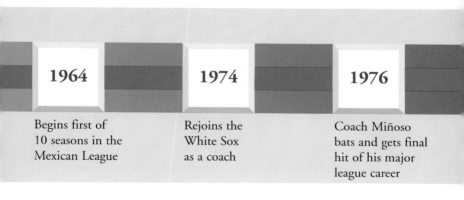

1964	1974	1976
Begins first of 10 seasons in the Mexican League	Rejoins the White Sox as a coach	Coach Miñoso bats and gets final hit of his major league career

sportsmanship: the quality of playing and behaving fairly
represent: to stand for

A Long Career

Miñoso had one of the longest professional baseball careers ever. He played more than 10 years in Cuba. Then he played more than 15 years in the major leagues. After that, he still wasn't done. Miñoso played for 10 more years in the Mexican League.

In 1976, the White Sox hired Miñoso as a coach. That year, the Sox even gave him another chance to bat. Miñoso was 53 years old. He got a hit!

Miñoso was also a coach for the White Sox.

Giving Back

Miñoso was a pioneer. He was the first Latino player to break the "color line." He brought a new style of baseball to the United States. He helped change the slower game of the 1950s into the faster, more exciting game we see today.

Miñoso was lightning fast and took risks. He dared the other team to try to throw him out. He used his blazing speed to score runs and make great plays. He also was graceful. Maybe most importantly, he was a team leader.

Miñoso's success led teams to look to Cuba and other Latin countries for more young players. Many of these young men became stars. Latino players had a big impact on baseball, in the 1950s and beyond.

---

pioneer: a person who goes before, opening up the way for others
graceful: having smoothness and ease of motion
impact: effect

— CHAPTER 3 —

A Time of Giants

"So did most of the best players come from Cuba, Abuelo?"

"Cuba always had very good players."

"But were they the best?"

"Well, I am a Dominican and I am proud of my country. Let me tell you about the best two players I ever saw."

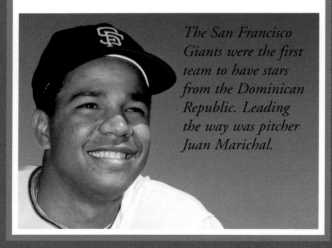

The San Francisco Giants were the first team to have stars from the Dominican Republic. Leading the way was pitcher Juan Marichal.

A Baseball Country

Today more U.S. major league players come from the Dominican Republic than from any other Latin country. That's not bad for a nation that has fewer people than Florida. How did it become the birthplace of so many major league stars?

Some say it started with Horacio Martinez. He had been a great player in the Dominican Republic. But the "whites-only" rule before 1947 shut him out of the major leagues.

When he was finished playing, Martinez became a coach. He wanted young people to have the chance he never got. In the 1950s, the San Francisco Giants hired him as a scout to look for players in the Dominican Republic. He sent the Giants several young men that became great players in the National League.

Horacio Martinez: (hor-AY-see-oh mar-TEEN-ez)

---

scout: someone who looks for players who might be able to be professionals

The Great Juan Marichal

Juan Marichal had a unique pitching style. He kicked his left foot so high that it went above his head. At times his hand dragged the ball so low, it almost touched the dirt.

Many teams wanted Marichal to play for them. But he was loyal to his friend, Martinez. The 19-year-old pitcher signed with the Giants in 1956 for $500.

Juan Marichal was the first Dominican to be elected into the Baseball Hall of Fame.

Juan Marichal: (wahn MAR-i-shal)

unique: not like any other
sign: to agree to play for a team

Climb to the Top

At first, Marichal played in small towns in the minor leagues. This life was sad and lonely for him. He missed the food and music of his home.

After less than two seasons in the minors, Marichal joined the Giants. In his first game, he struck out 12 players and gave up only one hit. It was the start of a great career.

Marichal won 191 games in the 1960s. No other pitcher won more. He was picked for the All-Star team nine times. Marichal was also named to the Baseball Hall of Fame in 1983. He was the first Dominican to receive this honor.

---

minor league: a group of professional baseball teams where athletes play to prepare for the major leagues

The Alou Brothers

Marichal wasn't the only player Martinez found. He also sent Dominican Felipe Alou to the Giants. Like Marichal, Alou had a hard time in the minor leagues. He did not know how to speak or read English. The first night he came to Florida, he did not know how to ask for a hotel room. He ended up sleeping on a park bench.

But after two years, Alou joined the Giants in 1958. He quickly became a star in the outfield.

Things were better when Alou's brother Mateo "Matty" joined the Giants in 1960. A third brother, Jesús, became a Giant in 1963. The Alou brothers played together in the outfield three times that year, but they would not be together for long.

Felipe Alou: (feh-LEEP-ay ah-LOO)
Mateo Alou: (ma-TAY-oh ah-LOO)
Jesús Alou: (hay-ZOOS ah-LOO)

The Alou brothers Felipe, Matty, and Jesús all played for the San Francisco Giants.

English Only

Several Giant players spoke mostly Spanish. They included Marichal and the Alou brothers. At shortstop, the Giants had José Pagan and at first base was Orlando Cepeda. Both were from Puerto Rico and spoke Spanish as well.

But the Giants manager, Alvin Dark, tried to make the players speak English. He felt having some players speak Spanish kept the team from acting like a group. The Spanish-speaking players became angry. It began to cause problems on the team.

José Pagan: (ho-ZAY pah-GAHN)
Orlando Cepeda: (or-LAN-doh sa-PAY-dah)

Split

In the 1960s, the Giants won more games than any team in their league. Still they did not win a World Series title. Dark, their manager, was fired. Some star players were traded.

The Giants traded Cepeda and the Alou brothers to other teams, where they did very well. Mateo Alou won the batting title for the Pittsburgh Pirates in 1966. Cepeda became a star in St. Louis. Felipe Alou later managed the Montreal Expos.

St. Louis Cardinals first baseman, Orlando Cepeda

batting title: award for highest batting average

A Giant Once More

In 2003, Felipe Alou became a Giant again. He was named manager of the Giants.

Alou is known as a good leader and teacher. He is also known for speaking out for Latino players. Alou believes that Latinos are not given a fair chance to coach and manage teams. As a manager and a spokesperson, Alou gives a lot back to Latinos in baseball.

San Francisco Giants manager Felipe Alou talks with players during spring training, February 2003.

spokesperson: a person who speaks for another or for a group

CHAPTER 4

The Great One

"You know a lot of players, Abuelo. Which one is your favorite?" Luis asked.

"There is one who stands above the rest. He was as good as any who ever lived, but he was also a great man and a true hero. His name was Roberto Clemente."

Roberto Clemente
(roh-BER-toh cluh-MEN-tay)

A Proud Man

When the 1971 World Series was over, reporters asked Roberto Clemente to speak. The Pittsburgh Pirates had beaten the Baltimore Orioles four games to three. Clemente was a big reason the Pirates had won.

Talking to millions, he spoke in Spanish. He thanked his parents and said it was the greatest day of his life. Clemente had many reasons to be proud.

He was a great hitter, one of the best ever. He was a speedy runner, on the bases and in the outfield. No one had a stronger throwing arm. He could hit the catcher's mitt from more than 400 feet (122 meters) away.

Clemente had hits in all seven games of the World Series, including two home runs. He helped win games with smart base running and great plays in the field. But even on this day, his thoughts were never far from the land of his birth and his family.

A Boy from Puerto Rico

Clemente was born in Carolina, Puerto Rico. He was the youngest of seven children. His father helped cut sugar cane and ran a small grocery store.

As a boy, Clemente played baseball with other children on sandlots. When he wasn't playing, he worked on his baseball skills. He squeezed a hard rubber ball to make his hands strong.

Roberto Clemente grew up in Carolina, Puerto Rico. There, his father helped cut sugar cane like the workers in this photo are doing. He also ran a small store.

---

sugar cane: the plant that sugar crystals come from
sandlot: sandy lots or fields where baseball is played

A Young Talent

As a teen, Clemente starred at track and field as well as baseball. His high school coach wanted him to try out for the Puerto Rican Olympic track team. But Clemente stayed with baseball, because that was what his father wanted him to do.

When Clemente was 17, a scout from the Brooklyn Dodgers saw him play at a tryout in Puerto Rico. Clemente played well and the Dodgers signed him for $15,000.

But the Dodgers already had great outfielders. So, in 1955, they traded Clemente to the Pittsburgh Pirates.

Roberto Clemente played for 18 seasons with Pittsburgh.

track and field: running, jumping, and throwing contests

A Tough Start

It was hard at first playing baseball in the United States. Clemente was lonely and homesick. Few people were friendly to the dark-skinned young man who could not speak English. Only two other players on his team spoke Spanish.

Some Americans did not like foreigners. One sportswriter called Clemente a "Puerto Rican hot dog." Some people made up their minds that Clemente was a bad player and a bad person. They didn't even know him.

This made Clemente angry. He was determined to show them the truth. The anger kept him working hard. He wanted his success to change the way people thought of him.

---

foreigner: a term for someone from another country
hot dog: a baseball term for someone who shows off too much
determined: firmly decided

Stardom

Soon fans began to see that Clemente was
a special player. In 1960, his fifth year with
the team, he helped the Pirates win the
World Series.

The next year, he led the league in hitting.
He also won the Golden Glove award as the
best fielder at his position. But Clemente's
life was more than baseball. He also visited
children in hospitals. He led sports programs
back home in Puerto Rico in the off-season.

Both on and off the field, Clemente did heroic things.

off-season: the time of year when a sport is not played

Success, Then Sadness

In the 1960s, Clemente played well. But it was not until Pittsburgh won the World Series of 1971 that people got to see how truly great he was. The next year, he got his 3,000th hit. At the time, he was the 11th player in the history of baseball to get 3,000 hits.

After the 1972 season, an earthquake struck the country of Nicaragua. Clemente wanted to help. On New Year's Eve, he got a plane to fly food and supplies to the people. The plane was so full that it crashed into the sea. Clemente died the way he had lived, giving his all.

Clemente spent 18 seasons with the Pittsburgh Pirates. He had a lifetime .317 batting average and won four batting titles.

ROBERTO WALKER CLEMENTE
PITTSBURGH N. L. 1955-1972

MEMBER OF EXCLUSIVE 3,000-HIT CLUB. LED NATIONAL LEAGUE IN BATTING FOUR TIMES. HAD FOUR SEASONS WITH 200 OR MORE HITS WHILE POSTING LIFETIME .317 AVERAGE AND 240 HOME RUNS. WON MOST VALUABLE PLAYER AWARD 1966. RIFLE-ARMED DEFENSIVE STAR SET N. L. MARK BY PACING OUTFIELDERS IN ASSISTS FIVE YEARS. BATTED .362 IN TWO WORLD SERIES, HITTING IN ALL 14 GAMES.

After Clemente

In 1973, Clemente was the first Latino elected to the Baseball Hall of Fame. That same year, baseball began to give the "Roberto Clemente Award" to a player known to help others.

In his lifetime, Clemente had helped others in many ways. He started a "sports city" for the youth of Puerto Rico. This is a place where young athletes can go to practice.

Roberto Clemente is remembered as one of baseball's finest players. The U.S. Postal Service issued a stamp in his honor.

With his skill and with his heart, Clemente showed baseball fans that Latino players are among the best in the world. He also showed how a truly great player gives back to others. He was an example to all.

---

heart: strong feelings and courage

— CHAPTER **5** —

The Best Ever?

"So, Luis, do you still think Miguel Tejada is the best ever?"

"Yes! But what do you think, Abuelo?"

"I think he has made his country proud. But I think you might even like him more if you knew how he got to be the player he is."

Tejada leaps over another player to make a double play.

Did You See That Play?

A ball is hit hard and low toward left field. The shortstop leaps and grabs the line drive. Then, still in the air, he pulls the ball from his glove and fires it to second base. Double play!

Plays like these come often for superstar Miguel Tejada. He can hit, run, throw, and field as well as any player alive. In 2002, Tejada helped lead his team to 20 wins in a row—a record for the American League. He was also named the league's Most Valuable Player.

line drive: a ball that is hit hard and straight
double play: baseball action in which two outs are made in a single play
field: to catch and return a batted ball

A Boy from Los Barancones

Tejada was born May 25, 1976, in Bani, the Dominican Republic. He was the youngest of 11 children. When he was 3 years old, a hurricane hit the Dominican Republic. The storm destroyed his family's house and all they owned. The Tejadas had to move to a shack without water or lights in a slum at the edge of the city.

Tejada's family was so poor that he could not go to school. At age 6, he had to help make money by shining shoes. But life was not only work for the young Tejada. Like many boys on the island, he loved baseball. Like them, he had dreams of playing in the big leagues.

hurricane: a powerful storm with high winds
slum: a very poor, run-down neighborhood

An Unlikely Star

As a boy, Tejada was short and very thin. He grew up without enough to eat. He wasn't even the best player in his own family. Many thought his older brother, Juansito, had more talent than Miguel. But Juansito broke his leg when he was a young boy. He ended up with a bad limp. There had been no doctor to help it heal properly.

Many boys in the Dominican Republic grow up dreaming of being great ballplayers.

Juansito: (wahn-SEE-toh)

Hard Work

There had been major league scouts on the island since the 1950s. U.S. teams wanted good, young players who did not ask for a lot of money. In the Dominican Republic, many people are poor. But baseball is a popular game there that anyone can play, rich or poor. For most, it ends up being just a game and not a career. For a lucky few, it is more. Tejada was one of those few.

As a teen, Tejada worked hard to improve his baseball skills. When he was 14, a coach named Enrique Soto saw that Tejada could play well. He helped guide Tejada to better understand baseball and to improve his skills.

Enrique Soto: (en-REE-kay SOH-toh)

A Fine Young Prospect

In 1993, when Tejada was 17 years old, Soto asked the Oakland A's to sign him.

The great Juan Marichal was the head of scouting in the Dominican Republic for the A's. He also thought Tejada was good. But neither Marichal nor Soto knew just how great a player this skinny teenager would turn out to be.

Tejada runs the bases. His speed, power, and hitting talent make him one of baseball's best all-around players.

prospect: a player who may turn out to be good some day

At the Top of His Game

Tejada rose fast in the minor leagues. He got his chance to join the major leagues in 1998. His hard work had paid off, but he kept learning and trying hard every day.

By 2000, Tejada was one of the league's top players. He hit 30 home runs that year and played very well in the field. The A's did not win the World Series, but they did win their division. Tejada had become a great player on one of baseball's top teams.

division: a group of teams that play each other

Baseball Belongs to the World

Since the days of Adolfo Luque, things have changed in North American baseball. It is no longer rare to see a Latino player. In the 2000 All-Star Game, one-third of the players came from Spanish-speaking countries. With determination, heart, fire, and style, many Latinos have become the leaders of their teams and superstars of the game.

So who is the greatest Latino player ever? Maybe he is yet to come.

Miguel Tejada signs a Dominican flag for a fan.

---

rare: uncommon

Epilogue

Here is a list of some of the best Latino baseball players in major league baseball history and where they were born.

UNITED STATES

Nomar Garciaparra	shortstop
Vernon "Lefty" Gomez	pitcher
Alex Rodriguez	shortstop

CUBA

Adolfo Luque	pitcher
Orestes "Minnie" Miñoso	outfielder
Tony Oliva	outfielder
Tony Perez	1st baseman
Luis Tiant	pitcher
Zoilo Versalles	2nd baseman

MEXICO

Beto "Bobby" Avila	2nd baseman
Fernando Valenzuela	pitcher

NICARAGUA

Dennis Martinez	pitcher

DOMINICAN REPUBLIC

Felipe, Mateo, Jesús Alou	outfielders
Juan Marichal	pitcher
Pedro Martinez	pitcher
Manny Mota	outfielder
Tony Peña	catcher
Manny Ramirez	outfielder
Sammy Sosa	outfielder
Miguel Tejada	shortstop

PANAMA

Rod Carew	1st baseman
Mariano Rivera	relief pitcher

PUERTO RICO

Orlando Cepeda	1st baseman
Roberto Clemente	outfielder
Bernie Williams	outfielder
Roberto Alomar	2nd baseman
Sandy Alomar, Jr.	catcher
Juan Gonzalez	outfielder
Ivan Rodriguez	catcher

VENEZUELA

Luis Aparicio	shortstop
Dave Concepción	shortstop
Omar Vizquel	shortstop

Glossary

ace closer: a team's best relief pitcher

amateur: done by people who play for fun,
  not money

batting title: award for highest batting average

deed: paper that shows that someone owns land

descent: ancestry

desire: a strong wish

determined: firmly decided

division: a group of teams that play each other

double play: baseball action in which two outs are
  made in a single play

field: to catch and return a batted ball

foreigner: a term for someone from another country

graceful: having smoothness and ease of motion

heart: strong feelings and courage

hot dog: a baseball term for someone who shows
  off too much

hurricane: a powerful storm with high winds

impact: effect

insult: a hurtful remark

line drive: a ball that is hit hard and straight

minor league: a group of professional baseball teams
  where athletes play to prepare for the major leagues

MVP (Most Valuable Player): an award given to a very
  important player

off-season: the time of year when a sport is not played

outfielder: the player whose job is to catch the ball near the back of the field

pioneer: a person who goes before, opening up the way for others

professional: done by people who are paid to play

prospect: a player who may turn out to be good some day

rare: uncommon

represent: to stand for

rookie: a first-year player in a league

sandlot: sandy lots or fields where baseball is played

scout: someone who looks for players who might be able to be professionals

sign: to agree to play for a team

slum: a very poor, run-down neighborhood

spokesperson: a person who speaks for another or for a group

sportsmanship: the quality of playing and behaving fairly

sugar cane: the plant that sugar crystals come from

take root: begin and start to grow

track and field: running, jumping, and throwing contests

triple: when a player reaches third base on a hit

unique: not like any other

Bibliography

Christopher, Matt. *At the plate with—Sammy Sosa.* Boston: Little, Brown, and Co., 1999.

Kingsbury, Robert. *Roberto Clemente.* Baseball Hall of Famers. New York: Rosen Publishing Group, 2003.

Muskat, Carrie. *Bernie Williams.* Latinos in Baseball. Childs, Md.: Mitchell Lane, 2000.

West, Alan. *Roberto Clemente: Baseball Legend.* Hispanic Heritage. Brookfield, Conn.: The Millbrook Press, 1993.

Useful Addresses

Major League Baseball
350 Park Avenue
New York, NY 10022

National Baseball Hall of Fame and Museum, Inc.
25 Main Street
Cooperstown, NY 13326

Negro Leagues Baseball Museum
1616 E. 18th Street
Kansas City, MO 64108-1610

Internet Sites

blackbaseball.com
http://www.blackbaseball.com/

Major League Baseball
http://www.mlb.com/NASApp/mlb/index.jsp

National Baseball Hall of Fame
http://www.baseballhalloffame.org

Science of Baseball
http://www.exploratorium.edu/baseball/

Index